ENGLISH

TIMED ASSESSMENT
PRACTICE TESTS

PRE-TEST

FOR 11+ AND 13+ ENTRY

Ages 10–12

ENGLISH PRE-TEST

FOR INDEPENDENT SCHOOL ENTRANCE

TIMED ASSESSMENT PRACTICE TESTS

FAISAL NASIM

Contents

ACKNOWLEDGEMENTS

Developed by Letts Educational in partnership with Exam Papers Plus (www.exampapersplus.co.uk) to benefit from their combined curriculum knowledge and assessment expertise.

The authors and publisher are grateful to the copyright holders for permission to use quoted materials and images.

'Christabel Pankhurst Transcript', www.bl.uk, with kind permission of The British Library

Going Solo, by Roald Dahl, © The Roald Dahl Story Company Limited. Published by Jonathan Cape Ltd and Penguin Books Ltd. Reproduced by permission of David Higham Associates Ltd.

Letters to my sister (of our experiences on our first trip to Europe, 1913), by Lilian McCarron

'Babies – learning starts for the first day', by Jennie Lindon, from the Learning together series, www.early-education.org.uk

Nineteen Eighty-Four, by George Orwell (Copyright © George Orwell, 1949). Reproduced by permission of Penguin Books Ltd.

The Great Events in History, by James Johonnot

Every effort has been made to trace copyright holders and obtain their permission for the use of copyright material. The author and publisher will gladly receive information enabling them to rectify any error or omission in subsequent editions. All facts are correct at time of going to press.

Published by Letts Educational
An imprint of HarperCollins*Publishers*

1 London Bridge Street
London SE1 9GF

ISBN: 978-1-84419-910-5

First published 2018

10 9 8 7 6 5 4 3 2 1

© HarperCollins*Publishers* Limited 2018

All rights reserved. No part of this publication may be reproduced, stored in a retrieval system, or transmitted, in any form or by any means, electronic, mechanical, photocopying, recording or otherwise, without the prior permission of Letts Educational.

British Library Cataloguing in Publication Data.

A CIP record of this book is available from the British Library.

Commissioning Editors: Michelle I'Anson and Alison James
Author: Faisal Nasim, Exam Papers Plus
Editor and Project Manager: Rebecca Skinner
Cover Design: Sarah Duxbury
Inside Concept Design, Text Design and Layout: Q2A Media
Production: Natalia Rebow
Printed in Great Britain by Martins the Printers

About this book

Pre-tests form part of the 11+ and 13+ admissions process at an increasing number of independent schools across the country. They are usually taken in Year 6 or 7, in an online, multiple-choice format. This book is designed to help students prepare for the English component of such tests.

Familiarisation with test-style questions is a critical step in preparing your child for any exams that they might be required to take as part of a school's assessment process.

This book provides your child with lots of opportunities to test themselves in short, manageable bursts, helping to build their confidence and improve their chance of test success. It contains 20 tests designed to develop key English exam skills.

- Each test is designed to be completed within a short amount of time. Frequent, short bursts of practice are found to be more productive than lengthier sessions.

- Pre-tests and similar assessments can be quite time pressured, so these practice tests will help your child become accustomed to answering the most frequently used question styles under timed conditions.

- We recommend that your child uses a pencil to complete the tests, so that they can rub out the answers and try again at a later date if necessary.

- Your child should complete the tests in a quiet place where they will not be disturbed. They will need a pencil and rubber to complete the tests. They will also need to be able to see a clock / watch.

- In the tests, an example is given for each question type to show your child what they must do.

- Test 1 is a complete test. Use this test to identify your child's strengths and weaknesses. Which skills and question types did they most struggle with?

- Tests 2–17 are grouped by skill / question type to provide focused practice. Cloze questions are used to test an understanding of grammar and vocabulary by asking children to choose the most suitable word or phrase to complete a sentence.

- Tests 18–20 are complete tests. By the time your child reaches these tests, you should be able to see an improvement in their confidence and results compared to Test 1.

- After completing Tests 18–20, your child should revisit any areas that need further work and attempt to improve their scores and timings.

- Answers to all questions are provided at the back of the book, with explanations where appropriate.

Read the passage and answer the questions that follow.
For each question, circle the letter next to the correct answer.

EXAMPLE

Adam applauded the diver as she stepped onto the podium to collect her Olympic silver medal.

In which sport did the athlete compete?

A   Rowing

B   Gymnastics

C   Hockey

(D)   Diving

E   Football

The following is an article about Christabel Pankhurst's Women's Suffrage Speech, published by the British Library.

The Christabel Pankhurst speech in 1908 is an interesting example of very early recorded speech. It's extremely rare – very few speeches were recorded before the First World War. And in fact, it's, I would probably think, fairly unusual for Pankhurst to be making a recording like this. She would have been much more used, as a leading feminist fighting for women's right to
5   the vote, to being outside in the open air on a street corner. This was a really important period for street corner oratory, long before radio and television began to have an impact. She would have been used to talking to huge crowds.

What we have in this recording is, I think, a slightly disappointing, rather scripted speech. There's something of the message there but it lacks the vigour and spontaneity that you would
10   expect from an outdoor speech of that particular time. For me, at least, it doesn't quite work. However, there are some interesting things that you can point out in the speech. Firstly, her accent, which is quite interesting – it's sort of quite posh. She uses, by our standards today, quite formal language. And most interesting, I think, is her determination to be very measured in her argument. And I think this is important because what she's effectively trying to do, I think, is to
15   counter the criticism that was very prevalent at the time aimed at Suffragettes – that they were sort of mad extremists. And she uses some very interesting phrases, notably when she says, "avoid the excesses of men", and I think that's a very important part of the speech.

Transcript

"The militant Suffragists who form the Women's Social and Political Union are engaged in the
20   attempt to win the parliamentary vote for the women of this country. Their claim is that those

women who pay rates and taxes and who fill the same qualifications as men voters shall be placed upon the parliamentary register. The reasons why women should have the vote are obvious to every fair-minded person.

25 The British constitution provides that taxation and representation shall go together. Therefore, women tax payers are entitled to vote. Parliament views questions of vital interest to women such as education, housing and the employment questions and upon such matters, women wish to express their opinions at the ballot box.

The honour and safety of the country are in the hands of Parliament. Therefore, every patriotic and public-spirited woman wishes to take part in controlling the actions of our legislators. For 30 forty years, this reasonable claim has been laid before Parliament in a quiet and patient manner. Meetings have been held and petitions signed in favour of votes for women but failure has been the result. The reason of this failure is that women have not been able to bring pressure to bear upon the government and government moves only in response to pressure.

Men got the vote, not by persuading but by alarming the legislators. Similar vigorous measures must 35 be adopted by women. The excesses of men must be avoided, yet great determination must be shown. The militant methods of the women today are clearly thought out and vigorously pursued. They consist in protesting at public meetings and marching to the House of Commons in procession.

Repressive legislation makes protests at public meetings an offence but imprisonment will not deter women from asking to vote. Deputations to parliament involve arrest and imprisonment 40 yet more deputations will go to the House of Commons. The present Liberal government profess to believe in democratic government yet they refuse to carry out their principles in the case of women. They must be compelled by a united and determined women's movement to do justice in this measure… [inaudible] …We have waited too long for political justice; we refuse to wait any longer. The present government is approaching the end of its career. Therefore, time 45 presses if women are to vote before the next general election. We are resolved that 1909 must and shall be the year of political enfranchisement of British women."

---

(1) What makes the recording of Christabel Pankhurst's speech so rare?

   A   Women almost never gave speeches.

   B   Christabel Pankhurst was considered a criminal.

   C   The speech was recorded before the First World War.

   D   Christabel Pankhurst was a celebrity.

   E   Speeches used to be rare occurrences.

(2) Which of the following had a negative impact on the importance of street corner oratory?

   A   The decline in temperatures

   B   The growth in popularity of radio

   C   New government legislation

   D   The growth in popularity of feminism

   E   The decline in travel by horse

Questions continue on the next page

(3) Which word best describes the writer's attitude to the speech?

    A   Excited

    B   Awed

    C   Shocked

    D   Disappointed

    E   Infuriated

(4) Why might this speech have felt different from Christabel Pankhurst's other speeches?

    A   She was forbidden from talking about certain topics.

    B   Her accent was too posh for a recording.

    C   The quality of the recording equipment was poor.

    D   She was accustomed to speaking outdoors to large crowds.

    E   She was rather shy.

(5) What were suffragettes often accused of?

    A   Extremism

    B   Deceit

    C   Terrorism

    D   Heroism

    E   Criminality

(6) What was the aim of Christabel Pankhurst's speech?

    A   To convince listeners of the need to end suffering

    B   To recount the history of the male voter

    C   To argue that women should be allowed to vote

    D   To persuade listeners to donate to charity

    E   To overthrow the government

(7) Why did Christabel Pankhurst refer to taxation in her speech?

    A   She believed that women should be exempt from taxation.

    B   She thought that taxes were too high.

    C   She wanted to eliminate some taxes.

    D   She believed that women should be allowed to vote if they paid taxes.

    E   She thought that those who paid taxes were inferior.

(8) According to Christabel Pankhurst, for how long had the campaign for suffrage been waged?

    A   Four decades

    B   One century

    C   Three years

    D   Thirty years

    E   Forever

(9) According to Christabel Pankhurst, what causes governments to take action?

A   Debate

B   Reason

C   Pressure

D   Generosity

E   Money

(10) Which party controlled the government in 1908?

A   The Labour Party

B   The Conservative Party

C   The Green Party

D   The Liberal Party

E   The Independents

(11) Which of the following is a synonym for 'vigour' (line 9)?

A   Heat

B   Vinegar

C   Weight

D   Energy

E   Pride

(12) Which of the following is an antonym for 'repressive' (line 38)?

A   Aggressive

B   Controlled

C   Tentative

D   Hopeful

E   Permissive

(13) What type of word is 'offence' (line 38)?

A   Noun

B   Adjective

C   Adverb

D   Pronoun

E   Verb

Questions continue on the next page

For each question, circle the letter below the group of words containing a spelling mistake.

If there is no mistake, circle the letter **N**.

The peeple at the festival enjoyed the party atmosphere as the moon rose overhead.

Ⓐ   B   C   D   N

---

(14) The judge decided to pass a lenient sentence due to the circumstances.

A   B   C   D   N

(15) The manager was unfortunately unable to accomodate the request.

A   B   C   D   N

(16) The tourist immersed herself in the language in an attemt to become fluent.

A   B   C   D   N

(17) Sacrafice still plays an important role in many global religions and cultures.

A   B   C   D   N

For each question, circle the letter below the group of words containing a punctuation or grammar mistake.

If there is no mistake, circle the letter **N**.

EXAMPLE

The fireworks reflected in the thames to produce a brilliant and colourful display.

  A   (B)   C   D   [N]

18 Where are we going today?" asked the young man as he packed his bag.

  A   B   C   D   [N]

19 Rachel and Andy each placed several precious stones in the container

  A   B   C   D   [N]

20 The flock of birds headed South to avoid the long and harsh winters.

  A   B   C   D   [N]

21 When he finished the project Bob decided to take a long and well-deserved break.

  A   B   C   D   [N]

Questions continue on the next page

For each question, circle the letter below the word or group of words that most accurately completes the sentence.

EXAMPLE

Finding a replacement | change | chart | chance | charge | charger | for her phone wasn't easy.
          A   B   C   D   (E)

(22) Two out of every three penguins in this region | is | were | being | is | are | currently
                 A   B   C   D   E

living on this beach.

(23) Wendy was excited as she | has | had | have | had not | hoped | never eaten that
            A   B   C   D   E

dish before.

(24) The people petitioned the queen to | showing | shows | showed | stop | show | mercy to
              A   B   C   D   E

the criminal.

(25) Most of the employees preferred to work | at | between | during | below | above |
                 A   B   C   D   E

the night.

Score: .... / 25

10

Test	# Comprehension
2	You have 14 minutes to complete this test.
	You have 10 questions to complete within the given time.

Read the passage and answer the questions that follow.
For each question, circle the letter next to the correct answer.

EXAMPLE

Adam applauded the diver as she stepped onto the podium to collect her Olympic silver medal.

In which sport did the athlete compete?

A Rowing

B Gymnastics

C Hockey

(D) Diving

E Football

The following is an extract from 'Going Solo' by Roald Dahl.

Somebody behind a desk in Athens or Cairo had decided that for once our entire force of Hurricanes in Greece, all twelve of us, should go up together. The inhabitants of Athens, so it seemed, were getting jumpy and it was assumed that the sight of us all flying overhead would boost their morale. So on 20 April 1941, on a golden springtime morning at ten o'clock, all
5 twelve of us took off one after the other and got into a tight formation over Elevsis airfield. Then we headed for Athens, which was no more than four minutes' flying time away.

Round and round Athens we went, and I was so busy trying to prevent my starboard wing-tip from scraping against the plane next to me that this time I was in no mood to admire the grand view of the Parthenon or any of the other famous relics below me. Our formation was
10 being led by Flight-Lieutenant Pat Pattle. Now Pat Pattle was a legend in the RAF. At least he was a legend around Egypt and the Western Desert and in the mountains of Greece. He was far and away the greatest fighter ace the Middle East was ever to see, with an astronomical number of victories to his credit. I myself had never spoken to him and I am sure he hadn't the faintest idea who I was. I wasn't anybody. I was just a new face in a squadron whose pilots
15 took very little notice of each other anyway. But I had observed the famous Flight-Lieutenant Pattle in the mess tent several times. He was a very small man and very soft-spoken, and he possessed the deeply wrinkled doleful face of a cat who knew that all nine of its lives had already been used up.

On that morning of 20 April, Flight-Lieutenant Pattle, the ace of aces, who was leading our
20 formation of twelve Hurricanes over Athens, was evidently assuming that we could all fly as brilliantly as he could, and he led us one hell of a dance around the skies above the city. Suddenly the whole sky around us seemed to explode with German fighters. They came down

on us from high above, not only 109s but also the twin-engined 110s. Watchers on the ground say that there cannot have been fewer than 200 of them around us that morning.

25 I can remember seeing our tight little formation all peeling away and disappearing among the swarms of enemy aircraft, and from then on, wherever I looked I saw an endless blur of enemy fighters whizzing towards me from every side. They came from above and they came from behind and they made frontal attacks from dead ahead, and I threw my Hurricane around as best I could and whenever a Hun came into my sights, I pressed the button. It was truly the

30 most breathless and in a way the most exhilarating time I have ever had in my life. The sky was so full of aircraft that half my time was spent in actually avoiding collisions. I am quite sure that the German planes must have often got in each other's way because there were so many of them, and that probably saved quite a number of our skins.

I remember walking over to the little wooden Operations Room to report my return and as I

35 made my way slowly across the grass I suddenly realised that the whole of my body and all my clothes were dripping with sweat. Then I found that my hand was shaking so much I couldn't put the flame to the end of the cigarette. The doctor, who was standing nearby, came up and lit it for me. I looked at my hands again. It was ridiculous the way they were shaking. It was embarrassing. I looked at the other pilots. They were all holding cigarettes and their hands were

40 all shaking as much as mine were. But I was feeling pretty good. I had stayed up there for thirty minutes and they hadn't got me.

They got five of our twelve Hurricanes in that battle. Among the dead was the great Pat Pattle, all his lucky lives used up at last.

---

(1) Where were the aeroplanes based?

  A   Italy

  B   Greece

  C   Germany

  D   England

  E   Egypt

(2) Why did the planes fly over the town?

  A   To assure and calm the locals

  B   To attack enemy aircraft

  C   To practise for combat

  D   Because the planes were on their way home

  E   Because the pilots were bored and needed something to do

3 How many Hurricanes were there?

A   10

B   8

C   12

D   6

E   2

4 Why couldn't the narrator admire the 'grand view of the Parthenon' (line 9)?

A   Because the Parthenon was in another city

B   Because there were clouds blocking the view

C   Because the Parthenon had been destroyed by enemy bombing

D   Because he was too focused on avoiding the other planes

E   Because the pilots were instructed not to look down

5 Which of the following best describes the narrator's attitude towards Flight-Lieutenant Pattle?

A   Jealousy

B   Fear

C   Anger

D   Indifference

E   Admiration

6 According to the narrator, why did Flight-Lieutenant Pattle appear to be sad?

A   He did not enjoy his job.

B   He was disappointed in the quality of the food.

C   He thought that he had experienced too many close calls already.

D   He missed his family.

E   He missed his deceased colleagues.

7 According to the narrator, why did so many of the Hurricane pilots remain alive?

A   They were skilled pilots.

B   The enemy pilots mistook them for allies.

C   The enemy pilots were outnumbered.

D   They were able to trick the enemy pilots and attack them by surprise.

E   The enemy pilots had to try to avoid each other.

Questions continue on the next page

(8) Why were the narrator's hands shaking?

    A   He had survived the flight and was in a state of shock.

    B   He was angry at having to report for duty.

    C   He was nervous about the idea of flying.

    D   He was excited about being a pilot.

    E   He had burnt his fingers with his cigarette lighter.

(9) '…he possessed the deeply wrinkled doleful face of a cat who knew that all nine of its lives had already been used up.' (lines 17–18)

What literary technique is used in this phrase?

    A   Simile

    B   Metaphor

    C   Alliteration

    D   Onomatopoeia

    E   Enjambment

(10) What type of word is 'exhilarating' (line 30)?

    A   Noun

    B   Adjective

    C   Adverb

    D   Pronoun

    E   Suffix

Score: .... / 10

Test	# Comprehension
3	You have 14 minutes to complete this test.
	You have 10 questions to complete within the given time.

Read the passage and answer the questions that follow.
For each question, circle the letter next to the correct answer.

EXAMPLE

Adam applauded the diver as she stepped onto the podium to collect her Olympic silver medal.

In which sport did the athlete compete?

A Rowing

B Gymnastics

C Hockey

(D) Diving

E Football

The following is an extract from the Arriva Trains Wales Passenger Charter.

Train cleanliness & facilities

We will clean the outside of our trains every two days and the inside at least once a day, where practicable, complemented by in-service cleaning.

We will not normally allow a train to enter service without a working toilet. A team of mobile
5 technical staff will be deployed to rectify faults that occur on trains in service wherever such repairs are possible.

Getting a seat

We plan our services so that you should usually be able to get a seat, although at peak times you may have to stand for a short period (typically less than 20 minutes). On certain
10 long distance services, particularly during busy periods, we would encourage you to make a reservation in order to be certain of getting a seat. We offer seat reservations on the majority of our longer distance services and details of these services are shown in our pocket timetables, which are available from staffed stations, our Customer Relations department or to downloaded from our website: www.arrivatrainswales.co.uk/timetables.

15 ### Punctuality and reliability

We aim to run all of our trains on time. We continue to strive to improve standards of punctuality and reliability, reviewing our performance standards annually.

We are committed to meeting Charter standards. Our performance figures for the previous four weeks and year will be available on posters at our staffed stations, on our website and from Customer Relations every four weeks. These figures are independently audited each year.

Performance figures of the other train operators who call at those staffed stations will also be available at the stations or on the other train operators' own websites.

Timetables

Timetable information will be displayed on platforms and concourses, and bilingual timetable booklets will be available free of charge at staffed stations, from our website or by post by telephoning Customer Relations on 03333 211 202. Timetable information will be available in alternative formats, including large type for visually impaired passengers by calling 03333 211 202.

At larger stations, information will also be provided by TV monitors, electronic information screens and public address systems.

Train Tracker

Train Tracker offers live arrival/departure board information over the phone.

For further information about these services please visit www.nationalrail.co.uk

Arriva Trains Wales app

Our app is the latest way to plan your journey to anywhere on the National Rail network and check live train running information for Arriva Trains Wales services. Download the app for free by searching "ATW Tickets" in your app store or visit app.arrivatrainswales.co.uk from your smartphone or tablet.

Information in advance of new timetables

When new timetables are introduced, copies of Arriva Trains Wales' timetables will be available at all staffed stations at least four weeks before the commencement of new services. Timetables can also be downloaded from the website. New timetable posters will be displayed at stations before the commencement of the new service. We will also display a summary of significant alterations to the train service four weeks in advance of each timetable change. In the case of planned engineering work, there will be at least seven days' notice of revised timetables and we will aim to keep any disruption caused by engineering works to a minimum.

(1) How often will the outside of the trains be cleaned?

   A   Once a week

   B   Twice a week

   C   Once a day

   D   Twice a day

   E   Three times a week

2 When will mobile technical staff be brought onto a train in service?

    A   When there is a fault that they can fix on the move

    B   When the train is on its last journey of the day

    C   When there are too many passengers on the train

    D   When the train needs cleaning

    E   Whenever a passenger requests support

3 How can one avoid having to stand on a long journey?

    A   By choosing to travel at an off-peak time

    B   By buying a special ticket whilst on the train

    C   By reserving a seat in advance

    D   By taking a different mode of transport

    E   By speaking with the driver

4 Which word best describes the writing in this extract?

    A   Fiction

    B   Descriptive

    C   Poetic

    D   Humorous

    E   Informative

5 Where can one check the reliability and punctuality of the company's trains?

    A   At any station

    B   In the local newspaper

    C   On the trains themselves

    D   Online

    E   It is not possible to check

6 Which of the following passengers would benefit from the Train Tracker service?

    A   A passenger requiring a hot meal on board

    B   A passenger looking for the toilet

    C   A passenger who wishes to know when the next train will depart from their station

    D   A passenger looking to upgrade to first class

    E   A passenger who wishes to cancel their booking

Questions continue on the next page

(7) On which of the following devices can the Arriva Trains Wales app be accessed?

   A   Tablet

   B   Desktop computer

   C   Laptop

   D   Television

   E   Radio

(8) How often are new timetables introduced?

   A   Every two weeks

   B   Never

   C   Once a week

   D   Annually

   E   We are not told.

(9) Which of the following is the best antonym for 'practicable' (line 3)?

   A   Unworkable

   B   Possible

   C   Inactive

   D   Realistic

   E   Abstract

(10) Which of the following is the best synonym for 'audited' (line 20)?

   A   Trialled

   B   Inspected

   C   Heard

   D   Contradicted

   E   Improved

Score: .... / 10

Read the passage and answer the questions that follow.
For each question, circle the letter next to the correct answer.

EXAMPLE

Adam applauded the diver as she stepped onto the podium to collect her Olympic silver medal.

In which sport did the athlete compete?

A   Rowing

B   Gymnastics

C   Hockey

(D)   Diving

E   Football

The following is an extract from 'Letters to my sister of our experiences on our first trip to Europe, 1913' by Lilian McCarron.

Friday, Aug. 23

Thursday was a very disastrous day for me; in fact, ever since we left New York we have faced a very strong wind from the east, and we encountered the severest since March — rather unfortunate to start with. However, it has cleared today and I am feeling all right. I went to bed
5   Wednesday at 9 and remained until Friday morning. I was not ill, but I couldn't sit up and feel comfortable, so the stewardess said if I felt better it would be just as well for me to lie down. But it didn't bother Tom at all. He is an A1 sailor, considering almost all on board were sick. He was able to put away his usual pile, promenade, and enjoy everything that was going. He is very busy in a game of deck quoits now, and he is enjoying it so much he is already speaking of
10   coming again.

To tell you something of the Mauretania, I might say the writing room and library is furnished with rosewood writing tables, chairs and couches, the latter upholstered in rose-coloured velvet, curtains in rose with Dresden border. This is the style all through the steamer.

The crew are all very attentive and they give the passengers the very best care, seeing that all
15   are comfortable with steamer rugs and feet raised off the floor when resting.

Someone was telling Tom it takes 1,800 pounds of bread a day to feed all, and five butchers to carve the beef.

So far I haven't met any of the passengers. There is one Toronto man on — G. Perry. He used to skate at Victoria and I think was connected with the Canadian General at one time.

20 On deck it is quite amusing to watch different styles worn. Mostly all the men wear cream flannel trousers and rubber-soled shoes. The ladies are fitted up as if on the board walk at Atlantic City.

In the furious storm blowing yesterday one of the lifeboats became unfastened, which meant the Mauretania had to stop her engines, change the course for some time in order to get it in place.

25 There was a heavy rain on Thursday night and this morning, and if you could see the mountainous waves the ship is ploughing through you wouldn't wonder she would be tossing. If I had been frightened I think I would have been real ill. I haven't been in the dining room since, but had lunch served to me on deck, as did all the people who were ill. Remaining in bed helped to keep me well. The lady in the stateroom next to us has been in bed ever since she came on.

30 She is suffering from nervous shock from a motor accident in which her husband, Mr Osgood Pell, was killed. Her maid is busy in attendance on her. A great many have maids and valets with them, while others keep the steward and stewardess busy. Ten minutes is allowed for bathing.

Sunday, Aug. 25

We have just come from having lunch, and Tom certainly put away a goodly share. Since leaving

35 New York he has been able to enjoy all his meals, and if he can relish them in the same quantity as he can take them it is some size. We have had almost all kinds of weather. While Saturday was a very beautiful day, it rained heavily at 7 p.m., and again Sunday morning, but since noon the sun has come out and the hazy atmosphere is clearing and all are enjoying the decks.

We attended, with a great many others, the Seamen's Orphanage aid concert in the second

40 class cabin last evening, which consisted principally of talent among the second class passengers, and afterwards the musicale in the lounge, and did not go to bed until 12 or a little later. Perhaps today we are more fortunate than unfortunate as all on board are talking about the narrow escape at 3 a.m. The 'Imperator', the new German liner, which is on its fourth trip, evidently lost something overboard and had lifeboats lowered just a half-mile off, which

45 is considered very close at sea, at the speed these steamers travel. The Mauretania gave the signal that she would take the starboard, but on approaching found the Imperator standing, which meant the Mauretania gave one quick turn on her side to avoid any damage, and many passengers were tossed out of bed. Tom and I slept so soundly we know nothing of it, and I think it was lucky for us we didn't.

(1) What caused Thursday to be a disaster?

A   An angry man

B   The wind from the east

C   Missing the boat

D   A shipping accident

E   An altercation with another passenger

(2) Why might the narrator have been envious of Tom?

   A   Tom was very rich.

   B   Tom did not have to eat.

   C   Tom won all the games he played.

   D   Tom was not affected by seasickness.

   E   Tom was very handsome.

(3) What is the Mauretania?

   A   A ship

   B   A train

   C   A car

   D   A lorry

   E   An aircraft

(4) From where was the narrator travelling?

   A   Atlantic City

   B   Ontario

   C   Victoria

   D   Liverpool

   E   New York

(5) What did the narrator enjoy doing whilst on deck?

   A   Reading a book

   B   Drinking a cocktail

   C   Conversing with fellow passengers

   D   Looking at what people were wearing

   E   Gazing out into the distance

(6) Which of the following statements is **true**?

   A   The weather was gentle and calm throughout the journey.

   B   The narrator was not unwell during the journey.

   C   Mr Osgood Pell died of natural causes.

   D   There were no second-class passengers on board.

   E   Tom ate large quantities of food.

Questions continue on the next page

7. What was the weather like on Sunday afternoon?

   A   Sunny

   B   Windy

   C   Hazy

   D   Rainy

   E   Freezing

8. What happened at 3 a.m.?

   A   Two steamers nearly ran into each other.

   B   People were sitting out on the deck.

   C   There was a dreadful accident.

   D   Everyone slept soundly.

   E   Two passengers began to brawl.

9. Which of the following is the best synonym for 'upholstered' (line 12)?

   A   Lifted

   B   Covered

   C   Furnished

   D   Painted

   E   Held

10. What type of word is 'soundly' (line 48)?

   A   Noun

   B   Adjective

   C   Adverb

   D   Verb

   E   Pronoun

Score: .... / 10

Comprehension

Read the passage and answer the questions that follow.
For each question, circle the letter next to the correct answer.

EXAMPLE

Adam applauded the diver as she stepped onto the podium to collect her Olympic silver medal.

In which sport did the athlete compete?

A   Rowing

B   Gymnastics

C   Hockey

Ⓓ   Diving

E   Football

The following is an extract from a leaflet, *Babies – learning starts from the first day*, by Jennie Lindon.

Taking care of a baby is tiring work, with a lot of feeding, nappies and broken nights. When you are exhausted, it can be harder to notice that a baby is really alert to what you do and say. It can be even harder if you have been told, 'Babies don't do anything' or 'They're not very interesting at first.'

5   But if you watch and listen to babies, you soon realise that people who say these things are missing so much.

Babies are learning from their first days. In fact, their brains are working before they are born, especially on seeing and hearing. You would not think there was much to see or listen to while babies are still developing in the womb. But by the end of pregnancy, light definitely filters
10 through to babies – and the womb is a noisy place.

Human babies are vulnerable. After they are born, they need good care just to survive. They cannot stagger to their feet like a newborn calf. But what they are missing in get-up-and-go, they make up for in brain power.

For instance:
15 •   Newborns are really interested in human faces and voices. Some clearly recognise their mother's voice. Babies are keen to be part of the social scene long before they produce 'proper' words.

•   Very young babies are able to copy the expression on your face. Sometimes they will even produce that expression a day later. They have remembered.

20   Practice makes perfect

Babies learn through repetition and by trying out lots of different ways to do the same thing. They actually build up connections in the brain with their keen practice in making trills of sound, playing with their toes or learning to crawl.

25 The world is all new to babies. So, in the first year of life, they find out that a toy dropped over the side of their high chair will make the same sound each time, but a cloth bib flutters down and does not make much sound when it touches the ground.

They like to have the same song from you or a peek-a-boo game with their older brother. This enthusiasm for 'again!' is spot on for their learning. Repeating the same thing helps them remember because it makes the unknown more familiar. A baby's broad smile shows you she
30 knows that a particular hand gesture you make means you are going to do 'Round and round the garden'. And happy repetition can help older children in the family too. A four-year-old big brother will be thrilled when 'my baby' starts the peek-a-boo game by waving the cloth in the air.

Babies learn to use their hands and mouth to explore. They put interesting things in their mouth because the nerve endings there are the most sensitive in their body. It makes no sense to try
35 to stop them. Just make double sure that anything they can reach is safe to suck. Babies use their current favourite action on anything. Holding, staring and mouthing are soon followed by tapping, shaking, poking or rubbing. Some actions, like dropping or throwing, can grow into a funny game with you or an older child as the fetcher.

Babies learn while you care for them

40 You do a great deal of care for babies so it is useful that they are keen to learn while you are feeding or changing them. Of course, you need to keep them safe on the changing mat or in your arms for breast or bottle feeding. But at the same time they are busy watching you while you feed them. They feel cherished by you and you are their safe place. Older babies want to use their physical skills to hold a cup or wave a spoon. Soon they will share in their dressing –
45 although a hat is as likely to be taken off as put on.

They listen to your words or singing as you change nappies and wet clothes. Babies as young as three months old can already join in through simple turn-taking. You say something and pause. They come back with sounds and gestures, then they pause. Amazingly, babies have already worked out the basics of a conversation. You help when you:
50 • are close to babies and make sure you have their attention
   • use ordinary words, keeping it simple, with short sentences
   • repeat what you say, with slight variations
   • are expressive with your tone and facial expression.

(**1**) Whom has this extract been written for?

   A   A teacher in a primary school

   B   An elected official

   C   A parent whose child has just started secondary school

   D   A parent of a newborn

   E   Nurses working in elderly care

② Which statement would the writer agree with?

    A   Babies are unable to comprehend much.

    B   Those who criticise babies should be imprisoned.

    C   Being tired can make it harder to notice a baby's awareness.

    D   Babies are not very interesting at first.

    E   Human babies are much more independent than calves.

③ Which senses are babies especially able to develop within the womb?

    A   Sight and touch

    B   Smell and sight

    C   Taste and smell

    D   Hearing and sight

    E   Taste and hearing

④ Why do babies place interesting objects in their mouths?

    A   Because they want to eat the objects

    B   Because they want to conceal the objects

    C   Because they want to feel and analyse the objects

    D   Because they want to bite the objects

    E   We are not told.

⑤ How do babies learn?

    A   By asking and answering questions

    B   By watching television

    C   Through repetition

    D   By wailing and coughing

    E   By observing and commenting

⑥ Which of the following is an optimal time for babies to learn?

    A   Whilst their nappy is being changed

    B   Very early in the morning

    C   Just after lunch

    D   When it is raining outside

    E   Just before they go to sleep

Questions continue on the next page

(7) Which word best describes the tone of this passage?

A   Pessimistic

B   Dismissive

C   Stern

D   Informative

E   Capricious

(8) Which of the following does **not** help babies develop their conversational skills?

A   Using clear and short words

B   Using exaggerated facial expressions

C   Making sure they are not distracted

D   Repeating words

E   Applying lotion to their hands and feet

(9) 'They cannot stagger to their feet like a newborn calf...' (lines 11–12).

What literary technique is used in this phrase?

A   Simile

B   Metaphor

C   Alliteration

D   Onomatopoeia

E   Rhyme

(10) Which of the following is a synonym of 'cherished' (line 43)?

A   Comfortable

B   Valued

C   Chastised

D   Obeyed

E   Denied

Score: .... / 10

Test	# Spelling
6	You have 7 minutes to complete this test. You have 12 questions to complete within the given time.

For each question, circle the letter below the group of words containing a spelling mistake.

If there is no mistake, circle the letter **N**.

EXAMPLE

The peeple at the festival enjoyed the party atmosphere as the moon rose overhead.

(A)   B   C   D   **N**

---

(1) The ranger was wary of the agressive bear that lived in the woods.

A   B   C   D   **N**

(2) Some of the attendees were furios about the band's outrageous behaviour.

A   B   C   D   **N**

(3) "It was never my intention to travel across the world with you," said the boy.

A   B   C   D   **N**

(4) The difference between sucess and failure is often quite minimal.

A   B   C   D   **N**

(5) The girl diluted the concentrate by pouring seven liters of water into the jug.

A   B   C   D   **N**

Questions continue on the next page

6) The new manager would tolerate neither arguement nor debate from staff or customers.

      A   B   C   D   N

7) Many did not aprove of the new measures because they thought they were too strict.

      A   B   C   D   N

8) The post office provides a valuable service, delivering letters promtly and cheaply.

      A   B   C   D   N

9) The sorcerers cowered in fear when they saw the ghastly omen in the sheep's entrails.

      A   B   C   D   N

10) His father was rather serious and stern; he rarley smiled or laughed.

      A   B   C   D   N

11) The plumber accidentally cracked a sewerage pipe, releasing a fowl odour into the room.

      A   B   C   D   N

12) The audience was boisterous and roudy so the comic knew he was in for a tough night.

      A   B   C   D   N

Score: .... / 12

Spelling

For each question, circle the letter below the group of words containing a spelling mistake.

If there is no mistake, circle the letter **N**.

EXAMPLE

The peeple at the festival enjoyed the party atmosphere as the moon rose overhead.

    (A)   B   C   D   N

① There is no margin for error when making such important calculations.

    A   B   C   D   N

② The police officer bellowed, "Stop right now or I will have to arrest you!"

    A   B   C   D   N

③ The commitee was responsible for deciding whether to approve the new project.

    A   B   C   D   N

④ Donkeys are renouned for their stubbornness, but they do not lack intelligence.

    A   B   C   D   N

⑤ The doctor was responsible for analysing patients and deciding if they were sain.

    A   B   C   D   N

Questions continue on the next page

6) The familar odour of smoke and sewago filled the air In the downtrodden village.

    A   B   C   D   N

7) She was fasinated by the peculiar design that had appeared on the wall overnight.

    A   B   C   D   N

8) The councillor ensured that the refugees were treated justly in the camp.

    A   B   C   D   N

9) The ruthless king beseiged the castle for two years before his enemies surrendered.

    A   B   C   D   N

10) The bank had no rules or regulations in place to deal with the calamaty.

    A   B   C   D   N

11) The teachers were determined to kerb any efforts to reduce their salary.

    A   B   C   D   N

12) A meager two-fifths of the population voted in the most recent election.

    A   B   C   D   N

Score: .... / 12

For each question, circle the letter below the group of words containing a spelling mistake.

If there is no mistake, circle the letter **N**.

EXAMPLE

The peeple at the festival enjoyed the party atmosphere as the moon rose overhead.

  (A)   B   C   D   N

---

(1) Try as he might, victory eluded the talented and brave cyclist for many years.

  A   B   C   D   N

(2) Only a fraction of the dinosaur's gigantic skeleton remains intact today.

  A   B   C   D   N

(3) The rulers considered all those who opposed them to be their mortal enemies and foes.

  A   B   C   D   N

(4) The waistful aristocrat spent an absurd amount of money renovating his bathroom.

  A   B   C   D   N

(5) "We recomend that you do not attempt to provoke the beast," advised the zookeeper.

  A   B   C   D   N

Questions continue on the next page

6 The soldeirs tried their hardest to revive their injured compatriot.

A   B   C   D   **N**

7 The earthquake brought about lasting damage, leaving many of the villagers destitute.

A   B   C   D   **N**

8 The old man feared that his power and influence were waining with age.

A   B   C   D   **N**

9 The historians were interested in investigating ancient hygienic practises.

A   B   C   D   **N**

10 The lawyer argued that her client was not liable for the restaraunt damage.

A   B   C   D   **N**

11 Light shone through the open windows and bathed the inteerior in a warm glow.

A   B   C   D   **N**

12 The wrestler refused to yield to his oponent, regardless of the circumstances.

A   B   C   D   **N**

Score: .... / 12

For each question, circle the letter below the group of words containing a spelling mistake.

If there is no mistake, circle the letter **N**.

EXAMPLE

The peeple at the festival enjoyed the party atmosphere as the moon rose overhead.

Ⓐ   B   C   D   N

---

① The vale was gradually lifted, revealing the intricate detail of the artist's work.

A   B   C   D   N

② Merchants and traders in Rome often lived interesting and prosperus lives.

A   B   C   D   N

③ The camel was no longer able to bare the weight of the sack that it was carrying.

A   B   C   D   N

④ Having joined her local golf club, she was obliged to pay anual membership fees.

A   B   C   D   N

⑤ A balanced combination of eggs and flour is required to make the desert.

A   B   C   D   N

Questions continue on the next page

6) The ship's captain expertly guided the vessel into the quiet harbour.

A   B   C   D   N

7) The stolen vehicle was brought to a halt when it collided with a stationery car.

A   B   C   D   N

8) Admision to the concert costs twice as much for adults than for children.

A   B   C   D   N

9) Every winter, the leaves on the tree wither away and dye as the weather gets colder.

A   B   C   D   N

10) The surgeon pioneered a novel techneek for performing knee operations.

A   B   C   D   N

11) The dispute between the warring neighbours had lasted for many decades.

A   B   C   D   N

12) The scientist was researching the relationship between industry and climate change.

A   B   C   D   N

Score: .... / 12

For each question, circle the letter below the group of words containing a punctuation or grammar mistake.

If there is no mistake, circle the letter **N**.

EXAMPLE

The fireworks reflected in the thames to produce a brilliant and colourful display.
    A   (B)   C   D   N

---

1 Although Sam lived in England, he was born in a spanish city called Seville.
    A   B   C   D   N

2 Before completing the puzzle, Lara decided to drink a cup of hot cocoa.
    A   B   C   D   N

3 The majority of the contributors to the journal were experts in, their field.
    A   B   C   D   N

4 To be successful, you will need to show courage grit and determination.
    A   B   C   D   N

5 The caring nurse asked the elderly patient, "How are you doing today."
    A   B   C   D   N

Questions continue on the next page

(6) George didnt believe his friends, so he decided to go and take a look for himself.

    A   B   C   D   **N**

(7) All of the cars engines had to be replaced due to the faulty electronics.

    A   B   C   D   **N**

(8) If you wish to visit the museum you must do so before it closes at five o'clock.

    A   B   C   D   **N**

(9) Jeremy bought three items from the shop: Gloves, a hat and a scarf.

    A   B   C   D   **N**

(10) The travellers continued heading West towards the magical waterfall.

    A   B   C   D   **N**

(11) The delighted man opened his arms to welcome his beloved dog, Wilson.

    A   B   C   D   **N**

(12) The aircraft landed very smoothly; the passengers' were all extremely relieved.

    A   B   C   D   **N**

Score: .... / 12

Grammar

You have 7 minutes to complete this test.

You have 12 questions to complete within the given time.

For each question, circle the letter below the group of words containing a punctuation or grammar mistake.

If there is no mistake, circle the letter **N**.

The fireworks reflected in the thames to produce a brilliant and colourful display.

    A   **(B)**   **C**   **D**   **N**

---

(1) "You really should'nt have done that!" exclaimed the boy. "We'll be in trouble."

    A   **B**   **C**   **D**   **N**

(2) The hungry tiger, who had not eaten for days prowled around the jungle.

    A   **B**   **C**   **D**   **N**

(3) Ellie wolfed down her beans as she was impatient for dessert – chocolate cake!

    A   **B**   **C**   **D**   **N**

(4) A steady stream of Japanese tourists visited the park throughout the Summer.

    A   **B**   **C**   **D**   **N**

(5) Whilst there are many possible explanations I think this one is the most likely.

    A   **B**   **C**   **D**   **N**

Questions continue on the next page

6 "Its important that we follow the instructions carefully," said the builder.

        A   B   C   D   **N**

7 Hardly any salmon remained in the river; many had been caught by fishermen

        A   B   C   D   **N**

8 Speaking loudly clearly and excitedly, the manager welcomed the new employees.

        A   B   C   D   **N**

9 Unaware of what was going on around her Paula continued to read her book.

        A   B   C   D   **N**

10 The young girl forgot to pack her new umbrella. However, it didn't rain.

        A   B   C   D   **N**

11 My favourite restaurant is in London; it's called the Sailor and serves seafood.

        A   B   C   D   **N**

12 Next year, my family and I plan to visit Berlin, which is the Capital of Germany.

        A   B   C   D   **N**

Score: .... / 12

For each question, circle the letter below the group of words containing a punctuation or grammar mistake.

If there is no mistake, circle the letter N.

EXAMPLE

The fireworks reflected in the thames to produce a brilliant and colourful display.

A   (B)   C   D   N

---

1. Wendy Jake, Layla, Dave and Ryan decided to go to the beach in the evening.

   A   B   C   D   N

2. If you are looking for a new job, fill out this questionnaire and we will help you?

   A   B   C   D   N

3. "Where are the other players?" Asked Jacky when she entered the changing room.

   A   B   C   D   N

4. Its highly unlikely that any of these plants will survive through the winter.

   A   B   C   D   N

5. Regardless of the circumstances such behaviour is completely unacceptable.

   A   B   C   D   N

Questions continue on the next page

(6) The football match was suspended as Oxford United's pitch were waterlogged.

A   B   C   D   N

(7) The pilot flew the Helicopter despite the weather warnings she had received.

A   B   C   D   N

(8) "There were four men in the group" said the witness to the police officer.

A   B   C   D   N

(9) The train will depart from King's Cross Station (Platform 7) at midday.

A   B   C   D   N

(10) Rudolf, Sam's pet Burmese python was coiled up in the corner of the room.

A   B   C   D   N

(11) The scientist's favourite experiment involved copper, acid and lots of water.

A   B   C   D   N

(12) Ending months of speculation, the company revealed it's new name: Hyperion.

A   B   C   D   N

Score: .... / 12

For each question, circle the letter below the group of words containing a punctuation or grammar mistake.

If there is no mistake, circle the letter **N**.

EXAMPLE

The fireworks reflected in the thames to produce a brilliant and colourful display.

    A   Ⓑ   C   D   N

---

① By late Autumn, most of the leaves on the trees have turned red, brown or orange.

    A   B   C   D   N

② Henry's mum's dog was ill so they made an appointment to see the Vet.

    A   B   C   D   N

③ What's the difference in price between these two sofas?" asked Gina.

    A   B   C   D   N

④ Many of the students werent able to complete the challenging exercise on time.

    A   B   C   D   N

⑤ The builder was not sure what to do about the supplies' that had been forgotten.

    A   B   C   D   N

Questions continue on the next page

(6) Four men, and one woman entered the building shortly after six o'clock.

A   B   C   D   [N]

(7) He usually visits me on thursdays, but he was unable to make it today.

A   B   C   D   [N]

(8) Henrietta Barley – the company's new president – was greeted warmly by all.

A   B   C   D   [N]

(9) The athlete credited her success to her husbands' unwavering belief in his abilities.

A   B   C   D   [N]

(10) The unruly passengers were asked to repair the seats in the new train's carriages.

A   B   C   D   [N]

(11) "Work harder!" yelled the miserable officer as he oversaw the troops

A   B   C   D   [N]

(12) My favourite month of the year is august because that's when I'm on holiday.

A   B   C   D   [N]

Score: .... / 12

Cloze

For each question, circle the letter below the word or group of words that most accurately completes the sentence.

EXAMPLE

Finding a replacement | change | chart | chance | charge | charger | for her phone wasn't easy.
A   B   C   D   (E)

① There are several ways | on | to | of | so | in | approach this problem.
     A   B   C   D   E

② Wendy removed the lettuce from all of | they're | there | their | thair | they are | burgers.
     A   B   C   D   E

③ Despite my protests, Rebecca insisted on paying | in | by | from | with | for | the meal.
     A   B   C   D   E

④ The flexible acrobat majestically dived | through | threw | throo | thorough | throw |
     A   B   C   D   E

the ring of fire.

⑤ I was | ate | eaten | eating | eat | eats | my sandwich when I heard the doorbell ring.
   A   B   C   D   E

Questions continue on the next page

(6) | Have | Having | Had | Halving | Half | completed his homework, Ben went outside to play.
  A   B   C   D   E

(7) Adam got stuck in traffic. | While | Furthermore | Because | Moreover | However |,
                               A   B   C   D   E

he had left early so he still arrived on time.

(8) They | where | were | was | are | is | unable to attend the party yesterday because
             A   B   C   D   E

they could not find a babysitter.

(9) " | Whose | Whos | Whom | Who's | Woe | fault is this?" demanded the
          A   B   C   D   E

infuriated manager.

(10) The teacher highlighted the importance of being kind | of | by | in | from | to | animals.
                                              A   B   C   D   E

(11) The plane flew | under | over | away | with | run | the city at night.
                     A   B   C   D   E

(12) Henry was an intelligent scientist and so his colleagues admired | her | his | hers | him | its |.
                                                      A   B   C   D   E

Score: .... / 12

Cloze

For each question, circle the letter below the word or group of words that most accurately completes the sentence.

EXAMPLE

Finding a replacement | change | chart | chance | charge | charger | for her phone wasn't easy.
                            A   B   C   D   (E)

(1) There were two crocodiles in the river; all the villagers feared
| it | their | them | his | her |.
  A   B   C   D   E

(2) There were far | than | to | too | two | tow | many containers waiting to be
                       A   B   C   D   E

loaded in the dock.

(3) Jane decided to write an | wild | surprising | curious | thrilling | exciting | children's story.
                                A   B   C   D   E

(4) Sarah wanted to put her new desk | on | between | nearby | at | in | the window
                                        A   B   C   D   E

and the door.

(5) Each of the contestants | was | are | of | were | will be | given a medal tomorrow.
                               A   B   C   D   E

Questions continue on the next page

(6) | Despite | Because | However | Furthermore | Moreover | Shane's lack of

      A   B   C   D   E

preparation, he managed to pass his driving test.

(7) There was little that could | of | have | having | had | over | been done to save

            A   B   C   D   E

the injured hare.

(8) " | Whomever | Whoever | Whichever | Wherever | Whatever | finds the egg

        A   B   C   D   E

will win a prize!" declared the teacher.

(9) "Don't | moved | moving | mover | movement | move |. I'll get help!" cried the

         A   B   C   D   E

man as he called the police.

(10) Ken was married | for | with | to | of | in | Hayley for a very long time.

          A   B   C   D   E

(11) Alison did her best to reason | about | for | with | on | by | the enraged criminal.

             A   B   C   D   E

(12) The soldier, | who has | whom | who had | which | whose | just returned home,

          A   B   C   D   E

was eager to rest and recuperate.

Score: .... / 12

Cloze

For each question, circle the letter below the word or group of words that most accurately completes the sentence.

EXAMPLE

Finding a replacement | change | | chart | | chance | | charge | | charger | for her phone wasn't easy.
              A   B   C   D   Ⓔ

---

1. Rachel and Edward both applied | about | | on | | for | | in | | to | the same job.
         A   B   C   D   E

2. | Odd | | But | | So | | Even | | Just | though Tom was careful, he was unable to avoid detection.
  A   B   C   D   E

3. Several of the | womans' | | womens | | womens' | | woman's | | women's | friends were
              A   B   C   D   E

   unable to attend her event.

4. The distance between the two runners increased
| great | | significantly | | largely | | significant | | impressive |.
 A   B   C   D   E

5. The scientist relied | in | | above | | on | | through | | for | the data to make her conclusions.
          A   B   C   D   E

Questions continue on the next page

6. "You and | you're | yore | youre | your | you are | uncle must come to visit," insisted Elena.
           A   B   C   D   E

7. The lawyer said, "Assuming | on | that | in | than | about | we can find a replacement,
                         A   B   C   D   E

you will be free to go."

8. Lizzie and her new puppy | were | is | was | werent | isn't | inseparable.
                        A   B   C   D   E

9. Despite the noise, William was able to | here | see | hear | touch | saw | the announcement.
                               A   B   C   D   E

10. Due | from | for | in | fore | to | his age, Ian was not allowed to watch the film.
        A   B   C   D   E

11. The accident looked catastrophic but the driver escaped serious
| health | growth | frown | injury | hurting |.
  A   B   C   D   E

12. Having already been to see the doctor, Frida had no option | but | in | of | accept | forced |
                                        A   B C   D   E

to wait.

Score: .... / 12

Cloze

<table>
</table>

Test 17

You have 7 minutes to complete this test.

You have 12 questions to complete within the given time.

For each question, circle the letter below the word or group of words that most accurately completes the sentence.

EXAMPLE

Finding a replacement | change | chart | chance | charge | charger | for her phone wasn't easy.
                  A   B   C   D   (E)

1. Rita ran through the rain as fast as she could but she could not avoid getting
| dry | rained | wet | soak | umbrella |.
 A   B   C   D   E

2. "| Who's | Whose | Who | Who'd | Whom | going to the factory?" asked Theresa.
   A   B   C   D   E

3. The lions | stealth | hungry | quicker | stealthily | steal | stalked the antelope.
      A   B   C   D   E

4. You can substitute honey | by | in | between | of | for | sugar in the recipe.
            A   B   C   D E

5. Two women | past | passed | pass | passing | paste | by the market and entered the park.
       A   B   C   D   E

Questions continue on the next page

49

6) Sarah's collection was larger than her [sisters] [sister] [sister's] [brothers] [fathers]
                                              A   B   C   D   E

collection.

7) The worker [expecting] [was expecting] [had been expect] [expectation]
                   A   B   C   D

[were expecting] to be paid more.
        E

8) The lady sat in the hospital and waited for her appointment with the
[teacher] [astronaut] [engineer] [doctor] [trader].
    A   B   C   D   E

9) Toby was determined to try as hard [if] [of] [with] [by] [as] he could.
                                        A   B   C   D   E

10) "He [don't] [doesn't] [dont] [doesnt] [do not] know the difference between them!"
          A   B   C   D   E

bellowed Emily.

11) Most of the [participant] [visiting] [visitor] [participating] [participants] did not
                     A   B   C   D   E

enjoy the experience.

12) More [than] [then] [thin] [those] [think] eight hundred cases remained unsolved.
           A   B   C   D   E

Score: .... / 12

50

Complete test

You have 25 minutes to complete this test.

You have 25 questions to complete within the given time.

Read the passage and answer the questions that follow.
For each question, circle the letter next to the correct answer.

EXAMPLE

Adam applauded the diver as she stepped onto the podium to collect her Olympic silver medal.

In which sport did the athlete compete?

A   Rowing

B   Gymnastics

C   Hockey

(D)   Diving

E   Football

The following is an extract from '1984' by George Orwell.

It was a bright cold day in April, and the clocks were striking thirteen. Winston Smith, his chin nuzzled into his breast in an effort to escape the vile wind, slipped quickly through the glass doors of Victory Mansions, though not quickly enough to prevent a swirl of gritty dust from entering along with him.

5   The hallway smelt of boiled cabbage and old rag mats. At one end of it a coloured poster, too large for indoor display, had been tacked to the wall. It depicted simply an enormous face, more than a metre wide: the face of a man of about forty-five, with a heavy black moustache and ruggedly handsome features. Winston made for the stairs. It was no use trying the lift. Even at the best of times it was seldom working, and at present the electric current was cut off during
10   daylight hours. It was part of the economy drive in preparation for HateWeek. The flat was seven flights up, and Winston, who was thirty-nine and had a varicose ulcer above his right ankle, went slowly, resting several times on the way. On each landing, opposite the lift shaft, the poster with the enormous face gazed from the wall. It was one of those pictures which are so contrived that the eyes follow you about when you move. BIG BROTHER IS WATCHING YOU,
15   the caption beneath it ran.

Inside the flat a fruity voice was reading out a list of figures which had something to do with the production of pig-iron. The voice came from an oblong metal plaque like a dulled mirror which formed part of the surface of the right-hand wall. Winston turned a switch and the voice sank somewhat, though the words were still distinguishable. The instrument (the telescreen, it was
20   called) could be dimmed, but there was no way of shutting it off completely. He moved over to the window: a smallish, frail figure, the meagreness of his body merely emphasised by the blue overalls which were the uniform of the Party. His hair was very fair, his face naturally sanguine,

his skin roughened by coarse soap and blunt razor blades and the cold of the winter that had just ended.

25 Outside, even through the shut window-pane, the world looked cold. Down in the street little eddies of wind were whirling dust and torn paper into spirals, and though the sun was shining and the sky a harsh blue, there seemed to be no colour in anything, except the posters that were plastered everywhere. The black-moustachio'd face gazed down from every commanding corner. There was one on the house-front immediately opposite. BIG BROTHER IS WATCHING

30 YOU, the caption said, while the dark eyes looked deep into Winston's own.

Down at street level another poster, torn at one corner, flapped fitfully in the wind, alternately covering and uncovering the single word INGSOC. In the far distance a helicopter skimmed down between the roofs, hovered for an instant like a bluebottle, and darted away again with a curving flight. It was the police patrol, snooping into people's windows. The patrols did not

35 matter, however. Only the Thought Police mattered.

---

(1) In which season did the events in this extract take place?

    A   Spring

    B   Summer

    C   Autumn

    D   Winter

    E   We are not told.

(2) At what time of day did the events in this extract take place?

    A   Early morning

    B   Late morning

    C   Early afternoon

    D   Late afternoon

    E   At night

(3) Which word best describes the smell in the hallway?

    A   Fresh

    B   Pleasant

    C   Odourless

    D   Fragrant

    E   None of the above

4 What was the weather like?

A Warm and sunny

B Cold and rainy

C Bright and windy

D Bright and hot

E Rainy and warm

5 Why did Winston take the stairs?

A He preferred the extra exercise.

B His varicose ulcer required him to do so.

C The lift was occupied.

D He only had to climb one flight of steps.

E The lift was not working.

6 What type of programme was most likely being played on the telescreen?

A A comedy

B A romantic play

C A news report

D A sports broadcast

E A gardening show

7 What shape was the telescreen?

A Rectangular

B Circular

C Cube-shaped

D Square-shaped

E Hexagonal

8 Which word best describes Winston's build?

A Muscular

B Weak

C Wiry

D Rotund

E Obese

Questions continue on the next page

(9) What did Winston see when he looked out of the window?

    A   A man with a rugged moustache

    B   A grey sky

    C   Snow lining the pavement

    D   His brother

    E   Posters showing a man's face

(10) Why was the helicopter hovering?

    A   It was trying to save fuel.

    B   It was unsure where to go next.

    C   It was spying on people through their windows.

    D   It was being blown back by the wind.

    E   It was searching for Winston.

(11) Which of the following is a synonym for 'depicted' (line 6)?

    A   Portrayed

    B   Hugged

    C   Concealed

    D   Distracted

    E   Distorted

(12) Which of the following is an antonym for 'distinguishable' (line 19)?

    A   Recognisable

    B   Extinguishable

    C   Unclear

    D   Destined

    E   Powered

(13) What type of word is 'smallish' (line 21)?

    A   Noun

    B   Adjective

    C   Adverb

    D   Pronoun

    E   Verb

For each question, circle the letter below the group of words containing a spelling mistake.

If there is no mistake, circle the letter N.

The peeple at the festival enjoyed the party atmosphere as the moon rose overhead.

(A) B C D N

---

14) The traveller had to ration his limited supplies as he still had a long way to go.

A B C D N

15) Both parties were united in their condemnation of racism and terrorism.

A B C D N

16) She loved nothing more than romeing around the countryside in autumn.

A B C D N

17) The brash pirate was known to visit the dilapidated tavern ocasionally.

A B C D N

Questions continue on the next page

For each question, circle the letter below the group of words containing a punctuation or grammar mistake.

If there is no mistake, circle the letter **N**.

The fireworks reflected in the thames to produce a brilliant and colourful display.

    A   (B)   C   D   N

---

(18) The electrician, who began work last week was welcomed by her colleagues.

    A   B   C   D   N

(19) Whether you agree with me or not, I expect you to except my decision.

    A   B   C   D   N

(20) The giraffe wandered over to the watering hole; he scanned the horizon before stooping to drink.

    A   B   C   D   N

(21) "The sun is supposed to come out this afternoon," assured the tour guide

    A   B   C   D   N

For each question, circle the letter below the word or group of words that most accurately completes the sentence.

Finding a replacement | change | chart | chance | charge | charger | for her phone wasn't easy.
  A   B   C   D   (E)

22 I think this jacket belongs | too | about | above | for | to | the lady who came into the
                                  A   B   C   D   E

shop yesterday.

23 The flight is scheduled to land | at | on | in | by | with | Belarus in exactly three hours.
                                     A   B   C   D   E

24 " | Go | Going | Went | Goes | Goe | now!" commanded the grumpy old musician
      A   B   C   D   E

as he picked up his instrument.

25 The volunteers made a | expensive | impressive | obvious | understated | concerted |
                           A   B   C   D   E

effort to raise as much money as possible.

Score: .... / 25

57

Complete test

You have 25 minutes to complete this test.

You have 25 questions to complete within the given time.

Read the passage and answer the questions that follow.
For each question, circle the letter next to the correct answer.

EXAMPLE

Adam applauded the diver as she stepped onto the podium to collect her Olympic silver medal.

In which sport did the athlete compete?

A   Rowing

B   Gymnastics

C   Hockey

(D) Diving

E   Football

The following is an extract from 'Ten Great Events in History' by James Johonnot.

ENGLAND'S POWER TO RESIST THE ARMADA.

And what of England and of her ability to resist this formidable attack? For a hundred years before the beginning of the sixteenth century, the civil wars of the Roses had desolated the country and put an end to national growth. For the next fifty years, and until the
5   commencement of the reign of Elizabeth, violence and bloodshed were so common that the population barely maintained its own. In 1588, the whole number of people in England and Wales was estimated at four million, about one third of the population of Spain.

But England possessed two elements of strength — her people, although differing in creed and often warring with one another, were intensely patriotic, and were united as one man against
10 a foreign foe; and the ships of England, manned by English crews and commanded by great captains — the legitimate successors of the old Vikings — dominated the seas. No enterprise was too hazardous for these hardy mariners to undertake, and no disparity of force ever induced them to pause. Philip was often wrought to frenzy as he saw these bold corsairs capture his treasure-ships and ravage his coasts in sight of his invincible but impotent armies.

15 The mode of attack which Philip determined upon consisted of two distinct but co-operative movements. A formidable army of invasion, under the Duke of Parma, the most experienced and skilful commander in Europe, was stationed at several ports in the Low Countries, opposite the British coast, from Dunkirk east. Innumerable transports were provided to convey this host across the Channel, and, once on English ground, an easy and triumphant march to London was
20 expected. The second part of the grand expedition consisted of an immense fleet of the largest

vessels ever built, under the command of the Duke of Medina Sidonia, which was to drive away the English ships and convoy the army of Parma to the English shore. This fleet was christened by the Spaniards "The Invincible Armada."

25 Philip hastened his preparations with all the energy he could command. In every port resounded the axe and hammer of the ship-builder; in every arsenal blazed the flames of busy forges. All of Spanish Europe echoed with the din of arms. Provisions were amassed in a thousand granaries; soldiers were daily mustered on the parade-grounds, drilled, and accustomed to the use of *arquebus* and cannon. Carts and wagons were built in hundreds for the conveyance of stores; spades, mattocks and baskets were got ready for the pioneers; iron and brass ordnance were
30 cast, and leaden shot melted in enormous quantities; nor were the instruments of torture — the thumb-screw and the 'jailer's daughter' — forgotten.

In 1587, the preparations were nearly complete and the Armada was about ready to sail, when a knowledge of its destination became known to Sir Francis Drake, the great English commander. Without considering the disparity of force, the old sea-king, with a fleet of swift-
35 sailing vessels, made a sudden descent upon the port of Cadiz, where the ships of the Armada were at anchor. Many of the larger vessels escaped by taking refuge under the guns of the forts, but the city was lit up by the blaze of one hundred and fifty burning ships, and the great enterprise was delayed for another year.

SAILING OF THE ARMADA.

40 But this disaster only called forth greater exertions. The maimed vessels were repaired, new ones were built, and at length one hundred and thirty-two ships, many of them the largest ever known at the time, were ready to sail. They carried three thousand guns and thirty thousand men. On May 3rd, the Armada sailed from the mouth of the Tagus, but a great gale dispersed the ships, and obliged them to put back into port to repair. It was not until July 12th that the
45 fleet finally sailed from Corunna on its mission of destruction, and to meet its fate.

To cope with this formidable force, the whole British navy could muster only thirty-six vessels, all much smaller than the largest of the Spanish ships. But, in consideration of the great danger, merchants and private gentlemen fitted out vessels at their own expense, and by midsummer a fleet of one hundred and ninety-seven ships was placed at the disposal of the British admiral.
50 In tonnage, number of guns, and number of men, the strength of the whole fleet was about one half that of the Armada.

(1) Why was England in a weak position at the beginning of the 16th Century?

A   Drought

B   Famine

C   Internal conflict

D   Immigration

E   Foreign invasion

Questions continue on the next page

(2) What happened to the population of England in the years before the reign of Elizabeth?

    A   It doubled in size.

    B   It decreased by half.

    C   It grew by half.

    D   It stayed almost the same.

    E   We are not told.

(3) According to the author, what two advantages did the English possess?

    A   Sarcasm and wit

    B   Bravery and wisdom

    C   Sailing skills and wealth

    D   Wealth and courage

    E   Patriotism and sea-faring skills

(4) Who was responsible for leading the ground invasion of England?

    A   Philip

    B   Elizabeth

    C   The Duke of Medina Sidonia

    D   Sir Francis Drake

    E   The Duke of Parma

(5) In preparation for their attack, where did the Spanish initially store their food?

    A   On parade-grounds

    B   On ships

    C   In forges

    D   In granaries

    E   Under the ground

(6) Why was the Spanish invasion delayed in 1587?

    A   The weather conditions were poor.

    B   The workers went on strike.

    C   An enemy attack weakened their forces.

    D   They struck a peace treaty with the enemy.

    E   King Philip decided was running out of money.

(7) In what way were many of the Spanish ships unique?

    A   They were the fastest ever known.

    B   They had the most powerful guns ever known.

    C   They were the largest ever known.

    D   They had the most skilled sailors.

    E   They had the most unique colours and designs.

8 In which season did the Spanish attack finally commence?

A Spring

B Summer

C Autumn

D Winter

E We are not told.

9 Who contributed the funds for the majority of the ships in the British navy?

A The government

B The French

C Citizens of the country

D Sailors

E The Spanish

10 What type of text is the passage?

A Biographical

B Fiction

C Instructional

D Historical

E Romance

11 Which of the following is the best synonym for 'disparity' (line 12)?

A Weakness

B Power

C Different

D Balance

E Inequality

12 What type of word is 'daily' (line 27)?

A Noun

B Adjective

C Adverb

D Pronoun

E Verb

13 Which of the following is the best synonym for 'maimed' (line 40)?

A Damaged

B Deserted

C Revived

D Marginalised

E Abolished

Questions continue on the next page

For each question, circle the letter below the group of words containing a spelling mistake.

If there is no mistake, circle the letter N.

EXAMPLE

The peeple at the festival enjoyed the party atmosphere as the moon rose overhead.

(A) B C D N

(14) My mother has asked me to run some erands for her today.

A B C D N

(15) The wizard carefully rolled up the scriptchure and placed it back in the cave.

A B C D N

(16) He was unfortunately unable to seccure an investment for his company.

A B C D N

(17) The govenor was known for treating all those around him with considerable contempt.

A B C D N

For each question, circle the letter below the group of words containing a punctuation or grammar mistake.

If there is no mistake, circle the letter N.

EXAMPLE

The fireworks reflected in the thames to produce a brilliant and colourful display.

A   (B)   C   D   N

(18) Here's my shopping list: Eggs, bread, milk, flour, tomatoes and onions.

A   B   C   D   N

(19) "There were seven geese on the pond yesterday", said the woman confidently.

A   B   C   D   N

(20) "Theres not much that can be done in this situation," consoled the doctor.

A   B   C   D   N

(21) Having cleaned the kitchen the maid went upstairs to dust the bedrooms.

A   B   C   D   N

Questions continue on the next page

For each question, circle the letter below the word or group of words that most accurately completes the sentence.

(22) The physicist agreed | in | about | with | up | of | everything I presented in my lecture.
           A   B   C   D   E

(23) I had not yet | **completed** | **completing** | **completion** | **complete** | **completes** | the
            A   B   C   D   E

assignment when the bell rang.

(24) You must come and visit me | **wherever** | **whenever** | **whichever** | **whatever** | **whoever**
              A   B   C   D   E

you are next in the country.

(25) "I would like to introduce you | of | by | in | for | to | my husband," said the astronaut.
             A   B   C   D   E

Score: .... / 25

Complete test

Read the passage and answer the questions that follow.
For each question, circle the letter next to the correct answer.

EXAMPLE

Adam applauded the diver as she stepped onto the podium to collect her Olympic silver medal.

In which sport did the athlete compete?

A   Rowing

B   Gymnastics

C   Hockey

(D)   Diving

E   Football

The following is an extract from 'The Jungle Book' by Rudyard Kipling.

All these things happened several years ago at a place called Novastoshnah, or North East Point, on the Island of St. Paul, away and away in the Bering Sea. Limmershin, the Winter Wren, told me the tale when he was blown on to the rigging of a steamer going to Japan, and I took him down into my cabin and warmed and fed him for a couple of days till he was fit to fly back
5   to St. Paul's again. Limmershin is a very quaint little bird, but he knows how to tell the truth.

Nobody comes to Novastoshnah except on business, and the only people who have regular business there are the seals. They come in the summer months by hundreds and hundreds of thousands out of the cold grey sea. For Novastoshnah Beach has the finest accommodation for seals of any place in all the world.

10   Sea Catch knew that, and every spring would swim from whatever place he happened to be in—would swim like a torpedo-boat straight for Novastoshnah and spend a month fighting with his companions for a good place on the rocks, as close to the sea as possible. Sea Catch was fifteen years old, a huge grey fur seal with almost a mane on his shoulders, and long, wicked dog teeth. When he heaved himself up on his front flippers he stood more than four feet clear of the
15   ground, and his weight, if anyone had been bold enough to weigh him, was nearly seven hundred pounds. He was scarred all over with the marks of savage fights, but he was always ready for just one fight more. He would put his head on one side, as though he were afraid to look his enemy in the face; then he would shoot it out like lightning, and when the big teeth were firmly fixed on the other seal's neck, the other seal might get away if he could, but Sea Catch would not help him.

20   Yet Sea Catch never chased a beaten seal, for that was against the Rules of the Beach. He only wanted room by the sea for his nursery. But as there were forty or fifty thousand other seals

hunting for the same thing each spring, the whistling, bellowing, roaring, and blowing on the beach was something frightful.

From a little hill called Hutchinson's Hill, you could look over three and a half miles of ground
25 covered with fighting seals; and the surf was dotted all over with the heads of seals hurrying to land and begin their share of the fighting. They fought in the breakers, they fought in the sand, and they fought on the smooth-worn basalt rocks of the nurseries, for they were just as stupid and unaccommodating as men. Their wives never came to the island until late in May or early in June, for they did not care to be torn to pieces; and the young two-, three-, and four-year-old
30 seals who had not begun housekeeping went inland about half a mile through the ranks of the fighters and played about on the sand dunes in droves and legions, and rubbed off every single green thing that grew. They were called the holluschickie—the bachelors—and there were perhaps two or three hundred thousand of them at Novastoshnah alone.

Sea Catch had just finished his forty-fifth fight one spring when Matkah, his soft, sleek, gentle-eyed
35 wife, came up out of the sea, and he caught her by the scruff of the neck and dumped her down on his reservation, saying gruffly: "Late as usual. Where have you been?"

It was not the fashion for Sea Catch to eat anything during the four months he stayed on the beaches, and so his temper was generally bad. Matkah knew better than to answer back. She looked round and cooed: "How thoughtful of you. You've taken the old place again."

40 "I should think I had," said Sea Catch. "Look at me!"

He was scratched and bleeding in twenty places; one eye was almost out, and his sides were torn to ribbons.

"Oh, you men, you men!" Matkah said, fanning herself with her hind flipper. "Why can't you be sensible and settle your places quietly? You look as though you had been fighting with the
45 Killer Whale."

"I haven't been doing anything but fight since the middle of May. The beach is disgracefully crowded this season. I've met at least a hundred seals from Lukannon Beach, house hunting. Why can't people stay where they belong?"

"I've often thought we should be much happier if we hauled out at Otter Island instead of this
50 crowded place," said Matkah.

"Bah! Only the holluschickie go to Otter Island. If we went there they would say we were afraid. We must preserve appearances, my dear."

Sea Catch sunk his head proudly between his fat shoulders and pretended to go to sleep for a few minutes, but all the time he was keeping a sharp lookout for a fight. Now that all the seals
55 and their wives were on the land, you could hear their clamour miles out to sea above the loudest gales. At the lowest counting there were over a million seals on the beach—old seals, mother seals, tiny babies, and holluschickie, fighting, scuffling, bleating, crawling, and playing together—going down to the sea and coming up from it in gangs and regiments, lying over every foot of ground as far as the eye could reach, and skirmishing about in brigades through
60 the fog. It is nearly always foggy at Novastoshnah, except when the sun comes out and makes everything look all pearly and rainbow-colored for a little while.

Kotick, Matkah's baby, was born in the middle of that confusion, and he was all head and shoulders, with pale, watery blue eyes, as tiny seals must be, but there was something about his coat that made his mother look at him very closely.

65 "Sea Catch," she said, at last, "our baby's going to be white!"

"Empty clam-shells and dry seaweed!" snorted Sea Catch. "There never has been such a thing in the world as a white seal."

"I can't help that," said Matkah; "there's going to be now."

1 Which of the following words best describes Limmershin?

   A   Aggressive

   B   Honest

   C   Sly

   D   Insecure

   E   Gallant

2 Why do seals congregate on Novastoshnah Beach?

   A   It is the closest beach to their usual home.

   B   It has the finest sand.

   C   It is hidden from predators.

   D   It is the only land available to them.

   E   It is the best place for seals to give birth to their young.

3 Which of the following locations is most prized among the married seals?

   A   The warm sand dunes

   B   The rocks close to the sea

   C   The rocks far back from the sea

   D   The sea close to the rocks

   E   The largest rock available

4 Which of the following words best describes Sea Catch?

   A   Proud

   B   Meek

   C   Perceptive

   D   Obliging

   E   Relaxed

Questions continue on the next page

(5) According to the extract, which of the following actions would contravene the Rules of the Beach?

    A   A seal attacking another seal at night

    B   A seal going for a swim during the daytime

    C   A seal using their teeth in combat

    D   A seal chasing after a beaten foe

    E   None of the above

(6) '…the surf was dotted all over with the heads of seals…' (line 25)

What does this phrase mean?

    A   Spots of foam from the sea clung to the seals' heads.

    B   Many of the seals had dotted markings on their heads.

    C   Seals with head injuries retreated into the sea.

    D   Rain fell heavily on the heads of the seals.

    E   There were many seals in the sea.

(7) According to the extract, why did the wives arrive at the beach later than their husbands?

    A   They often got lost along the way.

    B   They needed to tend to their children and this delayed them.

    C   They often decided to visit their friends before arriving.

    D   They lost track of time.

    E   None of the above.

(8) Which of the following statements is **true**?

    A   Sea Catch would have preferred to go to another beach.

    B   Matkah felt that Novastoshnah Beach was ideal.

    C   Sea Catch was concerned about what other seals thought of him.

    D   Matkah was furious with Sea Catch's behaviour.

    E   Sea Catch was a holluschickie.

(9) Which of the following best describes the usual weather conditions on Novastoshnah Beach?

    A   Rainy with occasional sun

    B   Foggy with occasional storms

    C   Foggy with occasional sun

    D   Sunny with occasional rain

    E   Sunny with occasional fog

10 "Empty clam-shells and dry seaweed!" (line 66)

Why did Sea Catch say these words?

A   To describe the state of the beach

B   To express annoyance that some seaweed was entangled in his flippers

C   To describe the only food they would have to eat

D   To express disbelief in response to Matkah's words

E   To express happiness in response to Matkah's words

11 What type of text is this passage?

A   Biography

B   Fiction

C   Non-fiction

D   Historical

E   Romance

12 Which of the following is the best synonym for 'unaccommodating' (line 28)?

A   Homeless

B   Brutal

C   Cooperative

D   Stubborn

E   Magnanimous

13 What type of word is 'cooed' (line 39)?

A   Noun

B   Adjective

C   Adverb

D   Pronoun

E   Verb

Questions continue on the next page

For each question, circle the letter below the group of words containing a spelling mistake.

If there is no mistake, circle the letter N.

The peeple at the festival enjoyed the party atmosphere as the moon rose overhead.

(A) B C D N

---

(14) The remoat island was inhabited by a wide variety of wild animals.

A B C D N

(15) The soldiers retreated hastily when they saw the size of the oposing force.

A B C D N

(16) The queen presided over the trial that sentenced the traiter to death.

A B C D N

(17) All medical students are taught the importance of implementing hygeinic practices.

A B C D N

For each question, circle the letter below the group of words containing a punctuation or grammar mistake.

If there is no mistake, circle the letter N.

EXAMPLE

The fireworks reflected in the thames to produce a brilliant and colourful display.

    A   (B)   C   D   [N]

---

(18) There were two different paths that we could have taken to reach my Village.

     A   B   C   D   [N]

(19) Several of the explorers' torches failed to function properly in the cavern.

     A   B   C   D   [N]

(20) The researcher was tired of dealing with the stress anxiety and politics in her workplace.

     A   B   C   D   [N]

(21) Last Summer, my family and I visited Hamburg, a city in northern Germany.

     A   B   C   D   [N]

Questions continue on the next page

For each question, circle the letter below the word or group of words that most accurately completes the sentence.

(22) "I don't approve | in | by | from | of | about | your decision," declared the furious commander.
               A   B   C   D   E

(23) | However | Although | Nevertheless | Despite | Moreover | it was still raining,
      A   B   C   D   E

Ben decided to go out and do some shopping.

(24) You | should have | should of | had to | must | should've | complete this task if you
           A   B   C   D   E

wish to be accepted in the group.

(25) Bella couldn't wait to get home and | drink | ate | devour | eaten | swallows |
                                A   B   C   D   E

her beef sandwich.

Score: .... / 25

Answers

Test 1 Complete test

Q1 **C** *The speech was recorded before the First World War.*

Q2 **B** *The growth in popularity of radio*

Q3 **D** *Disappointed*

Q4 **D** *She was accustomed to speaking outdoors to large crowds.*

Q5 **A** *Extremism*

Suffragettes were also accused of terrorism and criminality at the time. However, this is not mentioned in the text. The answers to comprehension questions must be based on information in the text.

Q6 **C** *To argue that women should be allowed to vote*

Q7 **D** *She believed that women should be allowed to vote if they paid taxes.*

Q8 **A** *Four decades*

'forty years' (line 30)

Q9 **C** *Pressure*

Q10 **D** *The Liberal Party*

Q11 **D** *Energy*

Q12 **E** *Permissive*

Q13 **A** *Noun*

The word 'offence' is a noun – it refers to a thing.

Q14 **N**

Q15 **C** *accommodate*

Q16 **C** *attempt*

Q17 **A** *Sacrifice*

Q18 **A** *"Where are we*

Q19 **D** *in the container.*

Q20 **B** *headed south to avoid*

Q21 **B** *project, Bob decided*

Q22 **E** *are*

present tense, plural

Q23 **B** *had*

past tense

Q24 **E** *show*

Q25 **C** *during*

Test 2 Comprehension

Q1 **B** *Greece*

Q2 **A** *To assure and calm the locals*

Q3 **C** *12*

Q4 **D** *Because he was too focused on avoiding the other planes*

Q5 **E** *Admiration*

'He was far and away the greatest fighter ace the Middle East was ever to see, with an astronomical number of victories to his credit.' (lines 11–13)

Q6 **C** *He thought that he had experienced too many close calls already.*

Q7 **E** *The enemy pilots had to try to avoid each other.*

Q8 **A** *He had survived the flight and was in a state of shock.*

Q9 **B** *Metaphor*

The words 'like' or 'as' are not used in the comparison, so it not a simile.

Q10 **B** *Adjective*

The word 'exhilarating' describes the 'time' (a noun).

Test 3 Comprehension

Q1 **E** *Three times a week*

'every two days' (line 2)

Q2 **A** *When there is a fault they can fix on the move*

Q3 **C** *By reserving a seat in advance*

This is the only option explicitly mentioned in the text.

Q4 **E** *Informative*

Q5 **D** *Online*

Figures are available on posters at staffed stations, not all stations, so A is not correct.

Q6 **C** *A passenger who wishes to know when the next train will depart from their station*

Q7 **A** *Tablet*

Q8 **E** *We are not told.*

Q9 **A** *Unworkable*

Q10 **B** *Inspected*

Test 4 Comprehension

Q1   **B**   *The wind from the east*

Q2   **D**   *Tom was not affected by seasickness.*

Q3   **A**   *A ship*

Q4   **E**   *New York*

Q5   **D**   *Looking at what people were wearing*

Q6   **E**   *Tom ate large quantities of food.*

Q7   **A**   *Sunny*

Q8   **A**   *Two steamers nearly ran into each other.*

Q9   **B**   *Covered*

Q10   **C**   *Adverb*

     The word 'soundly' describes how they slept (a verb).

Test 5 Comprehension

Q1   **D**   *A parent of a newborn*

Q2   **C**   *Being tired can make it harder to notice a baby's awareness.*

Q3   **D**   *Hearing and sight*

Q4   **C**   *Because they want to feel and analyse the objects*

Q5   **C**   *Through repetition*

Q6   **A**   *Whilst their nappy is being changed*

Q7   **D**   *Informative*

Q8   **E**   *Applying lotion to their hands and feet*

Q9   **A**   *Simile*

     The word 'like' is used to make a comparison, so it is a simile.

Q10   **B**   *Valued*

Test 6 Spelling

Q1   **B**   *aggressive*

Q2   **B**   *furious*

Q3   **N**

Q4   **B**   *success*

Q5   **C**   *litres*

Q6   **C**   *argument*

Q7   **A**   *approve*

Q8   **D**   *promptly*

Q9   **N**

Q10   **C**   *rarely*

Q11   **C**   *foul*

     The word 'fowl' is a homophone (sounds the same but has a different meaning). A fowl is a bird, especially one that can be eaten as food, such as a duck or a chicken.

Q12   **B**   *rowdy*

Test 7 Spelling

Q1   **N**

Q2   **N**

Q3   **A**   *committee*

Q4   **A**   *renowned*

Q5   **D**   *sane*

Q6   **A**   *familiar*

Q7   **A**   *fascinated*

Q8   **N**

Q9   **A**   *besieged*

Q10   **D**   *calamity*

Q11   **B**   *curb*

     The word 'kerb' is a homophone (sounds the same but has a different meaning). A kerb is the raised edge of a pavement.

Q12   **A**   *meagre*

Test 8 Spelling

Q1   **N**

Q2   **N**

Q3   **N**

Q4   **A**   *wasteful*

Q5   **A**   *recommend*

Q6   **A**   *soldiers*

Q7   **N**

Q8   **D**   *waning*

Q9   **D**   *practices*

     'Practice' is spelt with a 'c' when used as a noun and an 's' ('practise') when used as a verb.

Q10   **D**   *restaurant*

Q11   **C**   *interior*

Q12   **C**   *opponent*

Test 9 Spelling

Q1 **A** *veil*

The word 'vale' is a homophone (sounds the same but has a different meaning). A vale is a valley.

Q2 **D** *prosperous*

Q3 **B** *bear*

The word 'bare' is a homophone (sounds the same but has a different meaning). Something is bare if it is not covered.

Q4 **D** *annual*

Q5 **D** *dessert*

Q6 **C** *vessel*

Q7 **D** *stationary*

The word 'stationery' is a homophone (sounds the same but has a different meaning). Stationery is paper, envelopes and other materials or equipment used for writing.

Q8 **A** *Admission*

Q9 **C** *die*

The word 'dye' is a homophone (sounds the same but has a different meaning). If you dye something, you change its colour.

Q10 **B** *technique*

Q11 **N**

Q12 **N**

Test 10 Grammar

Q1 **C** *was born in a Spanish*

Q2 **N**

Q3 **D** *in their field.*

Q4 **C** *show courage, grit*

Q5 **D** *doing today?"*

Q6 **A** *George didn't*

Q7 **A** *All of the cars'*

A car has one engine, so 'cars' is plural and a possessive apostrophe should be positioned after the 's'.

Q8 **B** *visit the museum, you must*

Q9 **C** *shop: gloves,*

Q10 **B** *heading west*

Q11 **N**

Q12 **C** *passengers were*

Test 11 Grammar

Q1 **A** *"You really shouldn't*

Q2 **C** *days, prowled*

Q3 **N**

Q4 **D** *throughout the summer.*

Q5 **B** *many possible explanations, I*

Q6 **A** *"It's important that*

Q7 **D** *caught by fishermen.*

Q8 **A** *Speaking loudly, clearly*

Q9 **C** *her, Paula continued*

Q10 **N**

Q11 **C** *called The Sailor*

Q12 **D** *capital of Germany.*

Test 12 Grammar

Q1 **A** *Wendy, Jake, Layla,*

Q2 **D** *we will help you.*

Q3 **B** *other players?" asked*

Q4 **A** *It's highly unlikely*

Q5 **B** *circumstances, such*

Q6 **D** *pitch was waterlogged.*

Q7 **B** *the helicopter despite*

Q8 **B** *men in the group," said*

Q9 **N**

Q10 **B** *Burmese python, was*

Q11 **N**

Q12 **C** *revealed its new*

Test 13 Grammar

Q1 **A** *By late autumn, most*

Q2 **D** *see the vet.*

Q3 **A** *"What's the*

Q4 **B** *students weren't able*

Q5 **C** *to do about the supplies*

Q6 **A** *Four men and one*

Q7 **B** *on Thursdays, but he*

Q8 **N**

Q9 **B** *her success to her husband's*

Q10 **N**

Q11 **D** *the troops.*

Q12 **B** *the year is August*

Test 14 Cloze

Q1   **B** *to*
Q2   **C** *their*
Q3   **E** *for*
Q4   **A** *through*
Q5   **C** *eating*
Q6   **B** *Having*
Q7   **E** *However*
Q8   **B** *were*
Q9   **A** *Whose*
Q10 **E** *to*
Q11 **B** *over*
Q12 **D** *him*

Test 15 Cloze

Q1   **C** *them*
Q2   **C** *too*
Q3   **E** *exciting*

The word is preceded by 'an' so it must start with a vowel.

Q4   **B** *between*
Q5   **E** *will be*

future tense

Q6   **A** *Despite*
Q7   **B** *have*

'Could have' is correct. 'Could of' is sometimes incorrectly used because of the similarity in pronunciation between the two words when unstressed.

Q8   **B** *Whoever*

'Whoever' is used as the subject of a verb (as here); 'whomever' is used as the object of a verb, e.g. 'Bring whomever you like to the fair with you.'

Q9   **E** *move*
Q10 **C** *to*
Q11 **C** *with*
Q12 **C** *who had*

past tense

Test 16 Cloze

Q1   **C** *for*
Q2   **D** *Even*

Q3   **D** *woman's*

singular with a possessive apostrophe

Q4   **B** *significantly*

'Largely' means 'mainly' so is incorrect here.

Q5   **C** *on*
Q6   **D** *your*
Q7   **B** *that*
Q8   **A** *were*
Q9   **C** *hear*
Q10 **E** *to*
Q11 **D** *injury*
Q12 **A** *but*

Test 17 Cloze

Q1   **C** *wet*
Q2   **A** *Who's*

meaning 'who is'

Q3   **D** *stealthily*
Q4   **E** *for*
Q5   **B** *passed*

'Passed' is the past tense of 'pass', so is correct here. 'Past' is used for all other forms: noun, adjective, preposition and adverb, e.g. 'Two women walked past the market'.

Q6   **C** *sister's*

A possessive apostrophe is needed here.

Q7   **B** *was expecting*
Q8   **D** *doctor*
Q9   **E** *as*
Q10 **B** *doesn't*
Q11 **E** *participants*

A plural noun is needed here.

Q12 **A** *than*

Test 18 Complete test

Q1   **A** *Spring*

April

Q2   **C** *Early afternoon*

The clocks were striking thirteen (one o'clock).

Q3   **E** *None of the above*
Q4   **C** *Bright and windy*

Q5   **E**   *The lift was not working.*

Q6   **C**   *A news report*

Q7   **A**   *Rectangular*

            'Oblong' means 'rectangular'.

Q8   **B**   *Weak*

            Someone who is 'wiry' is thin but also strong, so it is not appropriate here.

Q9   **E**   *Posters showing a man's face*

Q10   **C**   *It was spying on people through their windows.*

Q11   **A**   *Portrayed*

Q12   **C**   *Unclear*

Q13   **B**   *Adjective*

            The word 'smallish' is used to describe his figure (a noun), so it is an adjective.

Q14   **N**

Q15   **N**

Q16   **B**   *roaming*

Q17   **D**   *occasionally*

Q18   **C**   *last week, was welcomed*

Q19   **D**   *accept my decision*

Q20   **N**

Q21   **D**   *assured the tour guide.*

Q22   **E**   *to*

Q23   **C**   *in*

            When talking about 'landing', 'in' is used for general locations (e.g. cities and countries), but 'at' can be used for more specific locations (e.g. Minsk National Airport).

Q24   **A**   *Go*

Q25   **E**   *concerted*

            The word is preceded by 'a', so it cannot begin with a vowel.

Test 19 Complete test

Q1   **C**   *Internal conflict*

Q2   **D**   *It stayed almost the same.*

            'the population barely maintained its own' (line 6)

Q3   **E**   *Patriotism and sea-faring skills*

Q4   **E**   *The Duke of Parma*

Q5   **D**   *In granaries*

Q6   **C**   *An enemy attack weakened their forces.*

Q7   **C**   *They were the largest ever known.*

Q8   **B**   *Summer*

            July 12th

Q9   **C**   *Citizens of the country*

Q10   **D**   *Historical*

Q11   **E**   *Inequality*

            'Disparity' is a noun, so the synonym must also be a noun. 'Different' can be used to describe a disparity but it is an adjective, so it is incorrect.

Q12   **C**   *Adverb*

            The word 'daily' describes 'mustered', which is a verb.

Q13   **A**   *Damaged*

Q14   **C**   *errands*

Q15   **C**   *scripture*

Q16   **C**   *secure*

Q17   **A**   *governor*

Q18   **B**   *shopping list: eggs,*

Q19   **C**   *yesterday," said*

            The comma should be inside the speech marks.

Q20   **A**   *"There's not*

Q21   **B**   *kitchen, the maid*

Q22   **C**   *with*

Q23   **A**   *completed*

Q24   **B**   *whenever*

Q25   **E**   *to*

Test 20 Complete test

Q1   **B**   *Honest*

Q2   **E**   *It is the best place for seals to give birth to their young.*

Q3   **B**   *The rocks close to the sea*

Q4   **A**   *Proud*

Q5   **D**   *A seal chasing after a beaten foe*

Q6   **E**   *There were many seals in the sea.*

Q7   **E**   *None of the above.*

Q8   **C**   *Sea Catch was concerned about what other seals thought of him.*

Q9   **C**   *Foggy with occasional sun*

Q10   **D**   *To express disbelief in response to Matkah's words*

Q11   **B**   *Fiction*

Q12   **D**   *Stubborn*

Q13   **E**   *Verb*

Q14 **A** *remote*

Q15 **D** *opposing*

Q16 **D** *traitor*

Q17 **D** *hygienic*

Q18 **D** *to reach my village.*

Q19 **N**

Q20 **C** *the stress, anxiety and*

Q21 **A** *Last summer, my*

Q22 **D** *of*

Q23 **B** *Although*

Q24 **D** *must*

Q25 **C** *devour*

Notes

Notes